A Murder of Crows

Written and illustrated by

Richard Metz

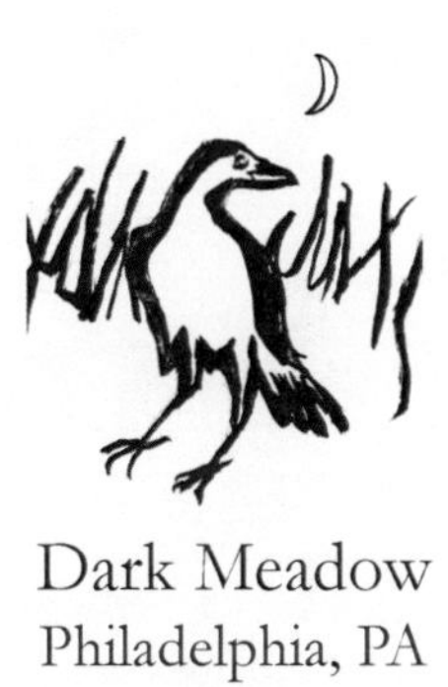

Dark Meadow
Philadelphia, PA

Published by Dark Meadow, 2024
Dark Meadow is an imprint of Frayed Edge Press

Cover image: Trouble in paradise
Back image: Arise from your slumber, Comrades

Library of Congress Control Number: 2024937179
ISBN: 9781642510553 (pbk.)

Book production and layout by Parlew Associates

Publishers Cataloging in Publication Forthcoming

Names: Metz, Richard.
Title: A murder of crows / written and illustrated by Richard Metz.
Description: Philadelphia, PA : Dark Meadow, 2024.
Identifiers: LCCN 2024937179 | ISBN 9781642510553 (pbk.)
Subjects: LCSH: Crows – Poetry. | Ravens – Poetry. | Crows – Art. | Ravens – Art. | BISAC: POETRY / Subjects &
    Themes / Animals & Nature. | ART / Subjects & Themes / Plants & Animals. | NATURE / Animals / Birds.
Classification: LCC N7666.R38 M48 2024 | DDC 704.9432 M--dc23
LC record available at https://lccn.loc.gov/2024937179

Table of Contents

Introduction

I'm excited to bring this book of poems and artwork to readers and viewers. It's the result of four years of drawing, painting, and writing. These poems and artworks are intended to be seen together, to create a deeper, more complex experience than either work separately. They are not meant to be illustrations of each other, but are rather paired creative works that illuminate each other.

Why crows? Well, I hear them every morning. Usually, they rest in the trees across the street, and swoop down after I walk outside and throw them peanuts. I'm sure they know so much more than I do about the specific flora and fauna of my home area. They are, for me, a symbol of the non-human, greater-than-human intelligence that surrounds me, in all the plants and animals.

Crows and ravens are serious birds. Their cries, caws, and cackles pierce the air, making humans cringe a little and take note. There is both a darkness and an omnipresence to crows in our lives. *A Murder of Crows* is a multi-faceted exploration of both the reality of and the myths about the crows and ravens that surround us.

This book has both images of graphite drawings and gouache paintings. The graphite drawings focus on crows and ravens in their present and historical realms. These works embody both the daily observations of crows outside my window, and my extensive readings on the habits and behaviors of corvids as well as the stories and myths that have grown up around them over the centuries.

Corvids (approximately forty-seven species of crows, ravens, and jackdaws) have followed the migrations of humans for thousands of years and are deeply imbedded in many mythologies as tricksters, agents of death, and intermediaries to other worlds. While there are differences among the corvids, with crows living closest to humans, science has shown that all corvids are intelligent, sociable among themselves, and interactive with humans and our society.

In the paintings, I've chosen to study and create images of crows as lead characters in the dramas that play out on the lands near me. I think that drawing and painting the land is also an excuse to be outside, studying nature for hours at a time. How miraculous are the movement of trees, the sounds of birds in the woods, the sun illuminating the meadow, the way natural forms grow and relate to one another! The art work then is a product of my time spent interacting with, breathing in, and wandering about these natural areas. But my love of the act of painting and drawing, creating lines, colors, and shapes, always takes over; I'm conscious of the fact that I'm not just studying the shapes of trees, leaves, and grasses, but creating compositions with color or tone, indulging in a kind of dancing, mark-making interplay with the natural world around me.

Working in the genre of landscape painting carries many codes and expectations based on the history of human interaction with the land. The places I've chosen to paint are preserved, purchased by governmental entities for the public good—a recognition of the value of natural areas to the health and welfare of humanity. All of this land was once part of the Lenape indigenous peoples' hunting grounds and was stolen from them as they were pushed out or killed.

Much of my work over the last thirty years has been focused on northwestern parts of Philadelphia and the surrounding areas, where I also grew up. My aspiration is that I can, with time, come to a deeper understanding, a closer emotional connection with the lands here. Due to the impact and consequences of my life here and the natural world's impact on me, I feel I am becoming part of this land, and the land a part of me.

My relationship with this area also entails responsibilities. I have been an environmental activist during these years as well, working to preserve the land from development, to protest sources of climate-destroying operations, gases, and chemicals, and to organize communities towards a more sustainable, healthier future for all—both humans and animals alike.

—Richard Metz
Philadelphia, 2024

Nature is red in tooth and claw

We consider in cozy white rooms
the angelic beauty of nature

Of all its creatures so great and
quite small,
each has purpose and plan
in the
Intricate infinite web

While out in the fields
and glens and cold hollows,
waft the wincing aroma
of blood

Limb pulled from limb,
and sinew from the bone,
each is rent
asunder

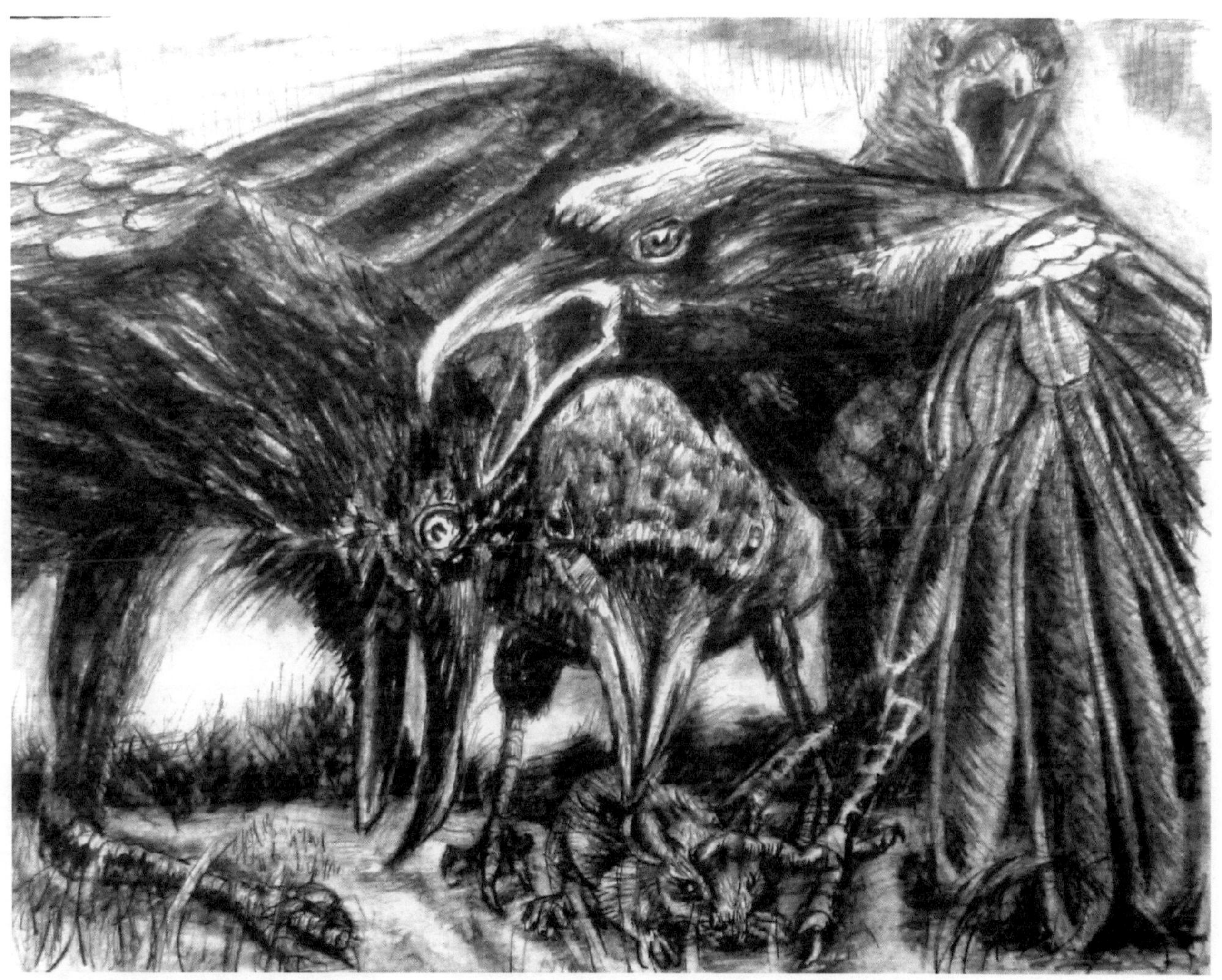

The Thicket

In the thicket we practice
covert maneuvers
to parry and lunge
plucking our meals

The cover provides
a gentle enveloping
A blind to wait
for oblivious prey

Blending with darkness
low to the ground
our beaks sharp and ready
for a prince's repast

Perhaps some beetle,
a worm or moth
but oh, yes oh
my kingdom for a mouse

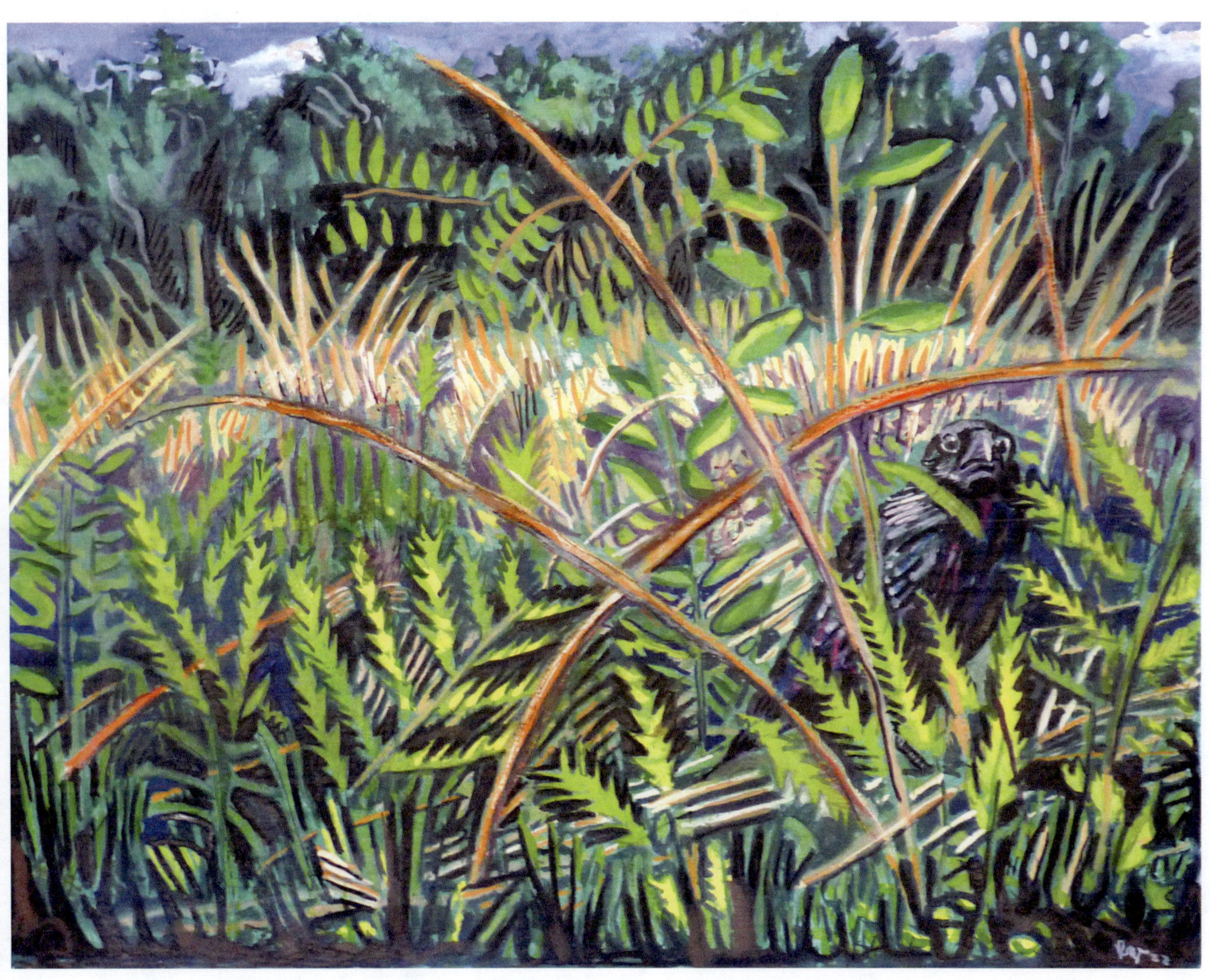

Inside and out

Who knows the scent
of sedge and stream
after unrelenting rains?

Who sees the Run
as it swells with showers
and overflows its banks?

Who glides over hill and crest
knowing the crevice between?
Who feels the branch
so brittle it breaks
in the stiff December wind?

And who falls to land one-last-time,
when our days have come to a close?

A difference of form is all,
symbiotic and entangled,
Love and its consequences

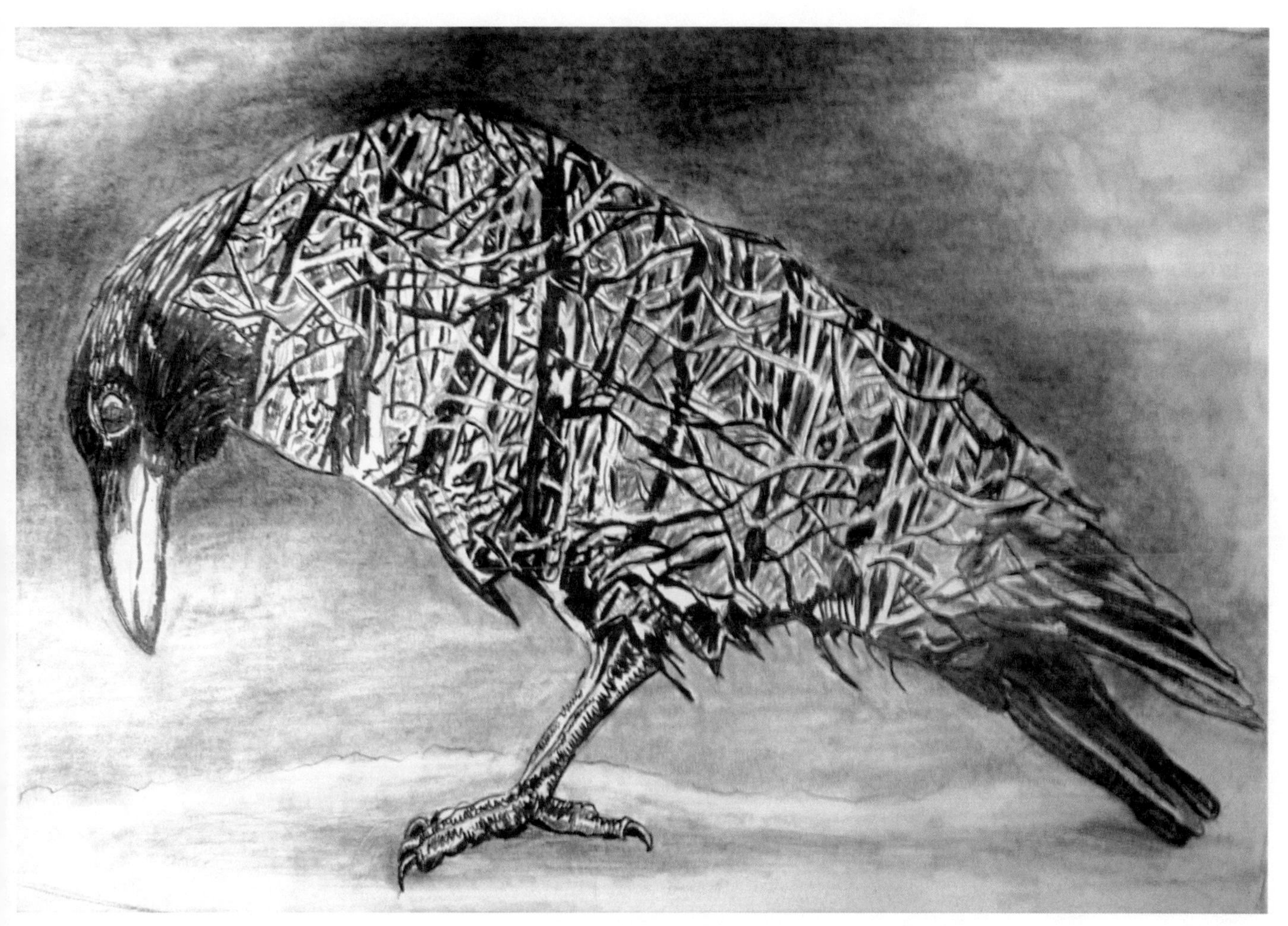

Autumn rushes in

Ahhhhh, yellow, Yell-o.
Leaves flying, fluttering palegolden
citrus buoyant sun,
over tall reeds and loosestrife,
all around yel-low
forever and ever

Indulge us Crows who come to see and feel
chortle chortle, caww caw caw,
surrounded by saffron amber, honey in lemon
marigold wine.
In the fluttering festival we alight,
in the endless smiling
eternal cyclical autumnal
oh Song of Songs

Those leaves, rubbing and rustling and sailing the sky
encompassing all in warm devotion.
Now, in flies the Crow, eater of light
darkness swooping
parting the woods, all around the colors of fire.
Solid light, bold light, sensate, pushing and pulling,
calling us…
put down your burdens and sorrows
and dance, just
daa da da, daa da da dance,
to the brief-long melody
of Autumn

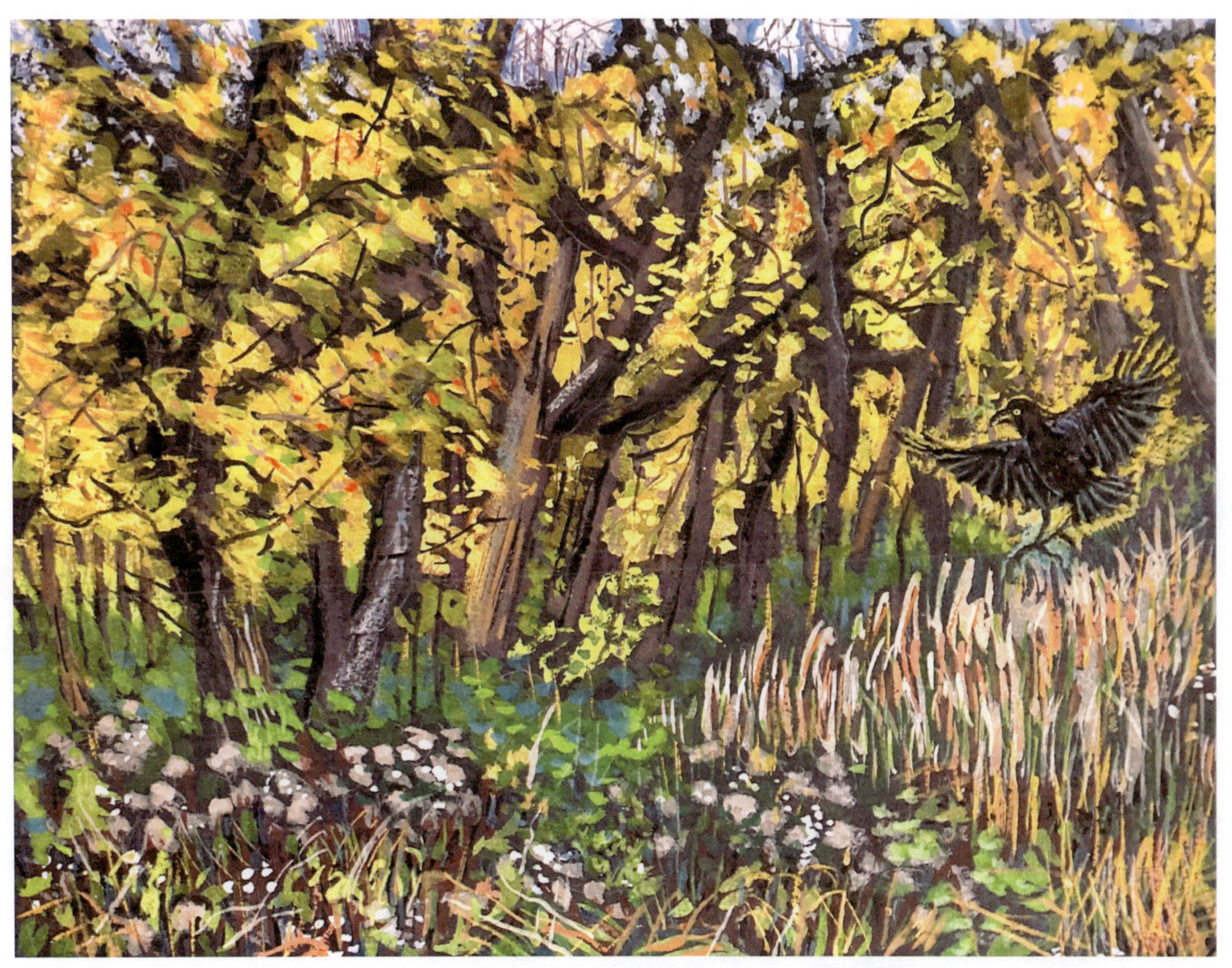

Departed Friend

Each morning we set out
for the generous fields
watching the July sun
Rise and fall, rise and fall.

But what's this now
we puzzle aloud:
some kind of living
Scarecrow?

Each day by nine, his calls and groans
aroused us from our glad tidings.
he yells and dances
rages and curses,
and waves that strange colored stick.
His yellow straw hat sails far away
in the hot Provençal winds.

He and we, and the waving wheat,
we miss him even still

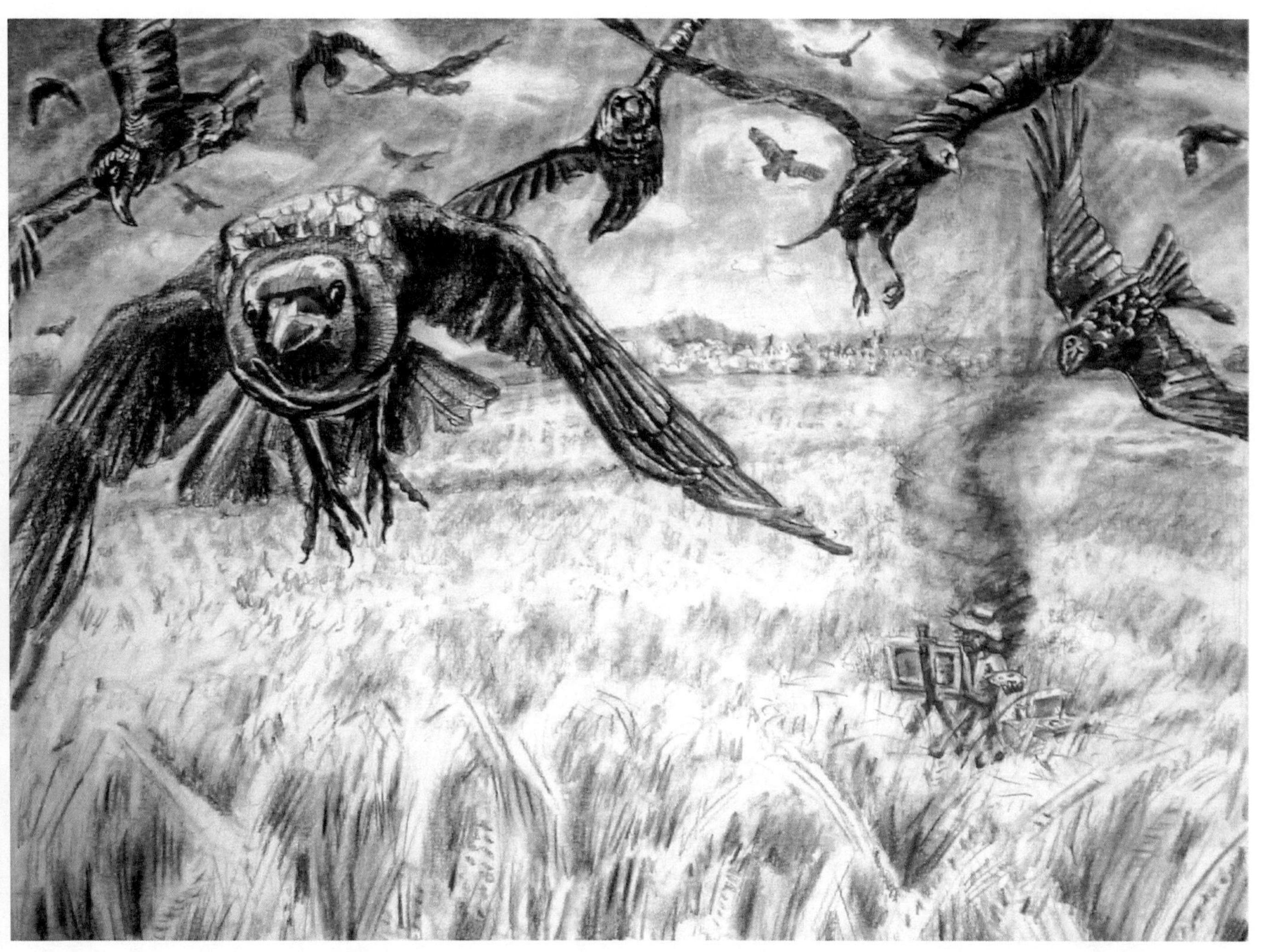

Mad Autumn

Mad autumn is here
run with abandon
grasses and leaves tear at the sky
flame mad colors and warm winds cool
spiraling our brains
pulsing our veins

The sky's falling sky dances,
red below and above,
yesterday's greens
a mere passing mirage,
grasses shoot up with yellow and white
higher and higher than even the trees
Mad autumn is wildly, utterly, madly
finally upon us

We can't slake our thirst
for pigment and light,
come burn inside
burn bright as the night,
Come down, come now
from your airy white cloud
and runmad with us monsters
in autumn's delight

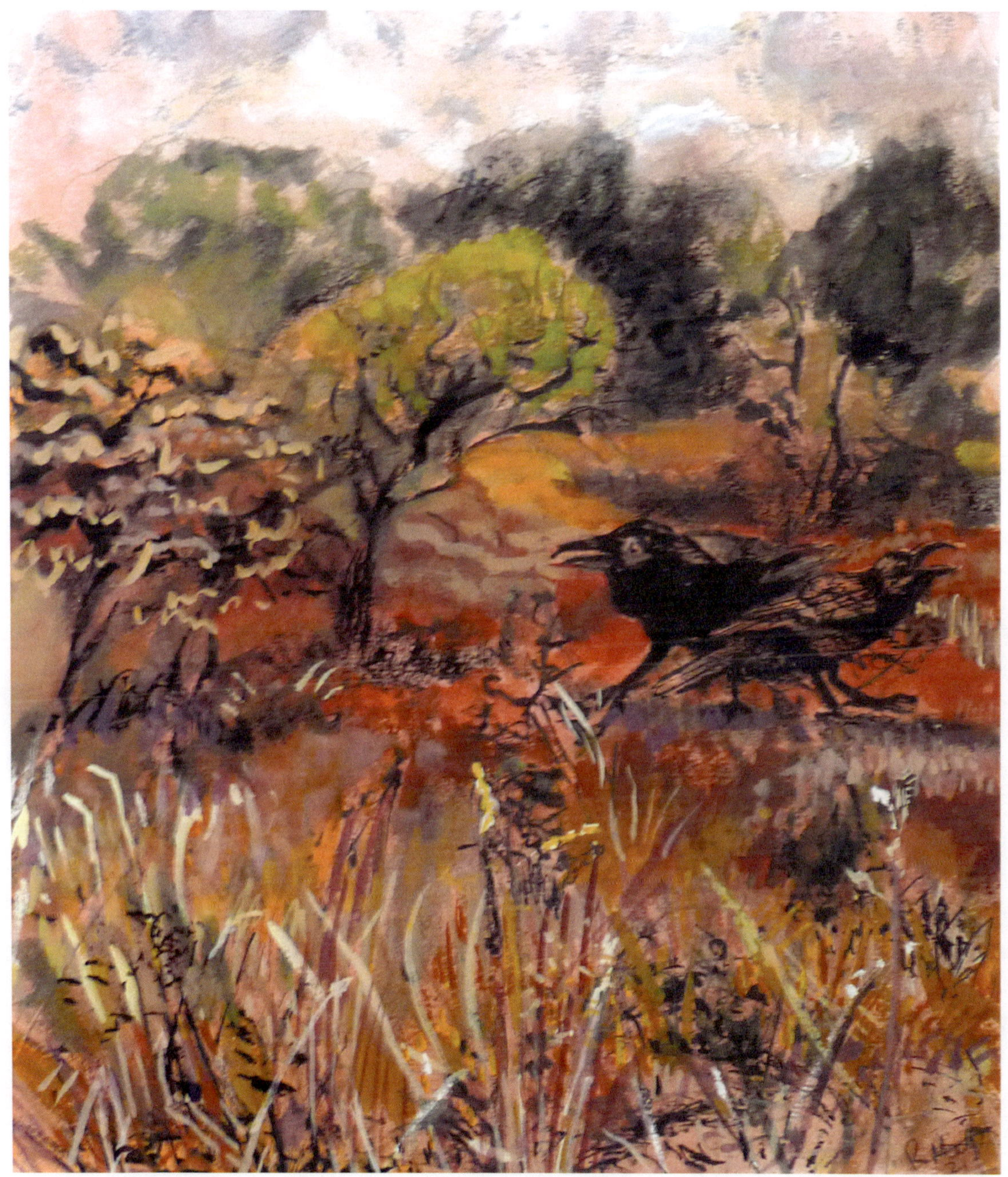

Morrigan

And what does it
feel like your highness?

To have claw for toe, wing for arm?
to feel oh feel
quick air rushing past you,
as you make your avian climb?

And what becomes of thoughts,
when beak extends from your lips?
Does it tingle or buzz
or hurt you inside,
when your bones take on
such a shape?

And will you take kindly to
all of our questions,
such personal matters for you?
Or will you send us
curling and lapping,
to the soil and the deep?

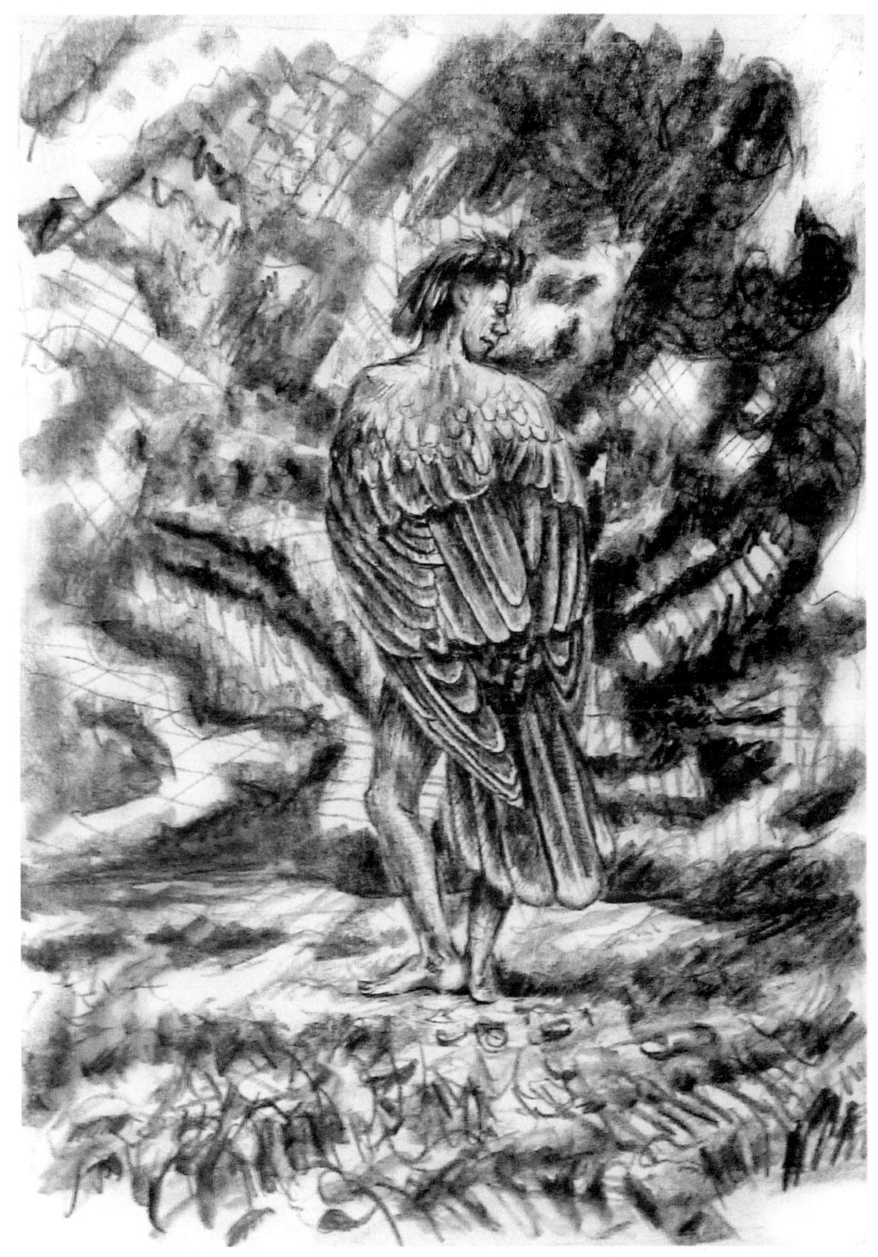

Golden hour

The golden hour
is here and upon us
let it inside, give up your fear
Time n'er passes
time under-foot

The golden hour
colors our dreams
remember when
at amber's lastglow,
Was there more for the wanting
even a moment for nought?

All here, all's near
my heart dread and bright cheer
make it stay, don't leave
not yet memory's domain.
But like flux and phlox
it's gone in a flash
till next we love next
gold Autumn

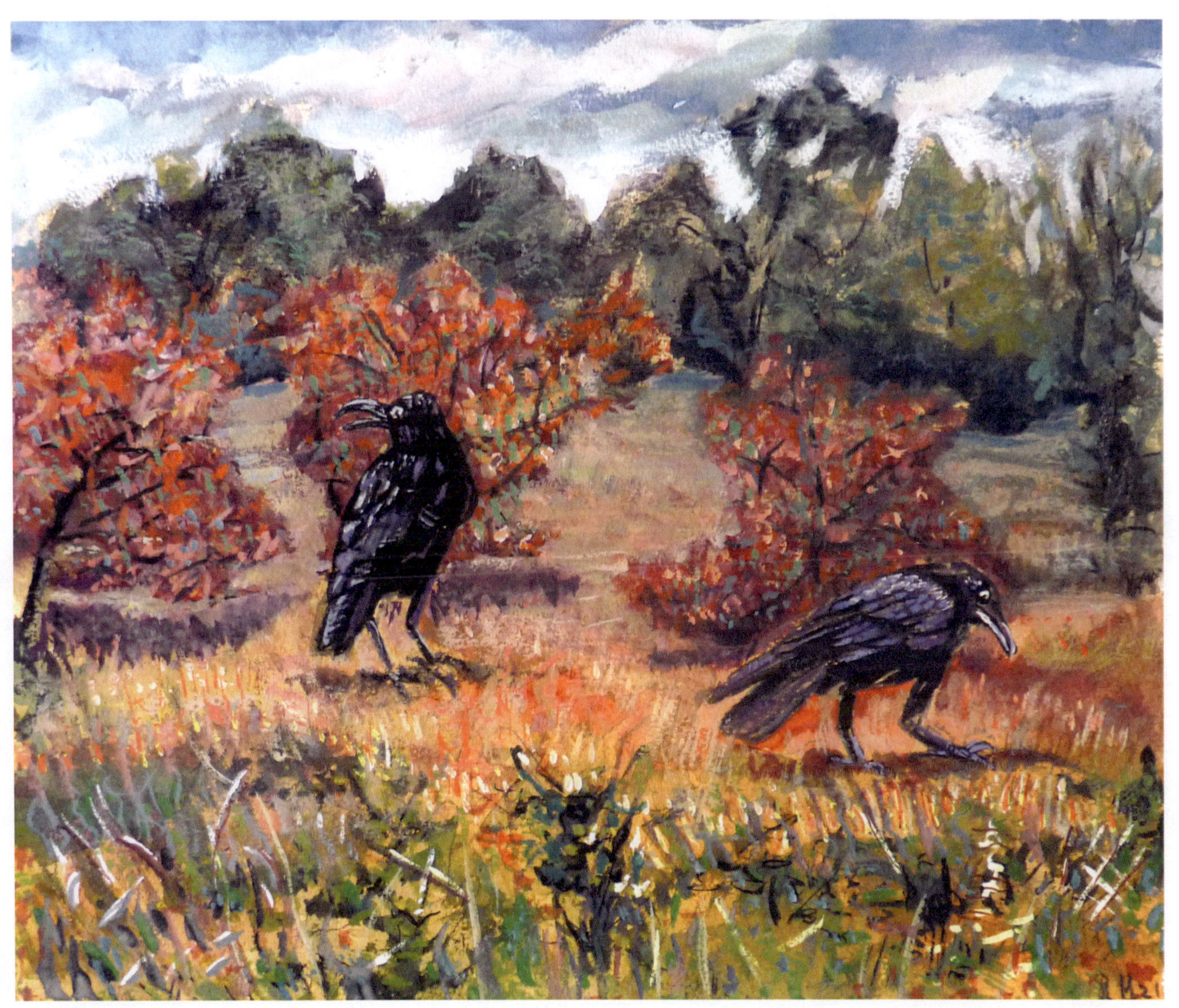

Funeral for a friend

We gather round departed Bill
no one made the call.
we sensed it like
an absent voice
a hole where there once
was none

He had a long
and querulous life
his cries were heard by all
they filled the air
like trumpets awry
mad with sympathy

How many years
we couldn't say
seasons passed
cold and warm.
new ones were born
elders die out

What brought him down
was nothing new
perhaps old age
a single tick
a bit of poison
or avian flu

His children are here
and spouses too
friends of friends
we gather round,
here to mourn
the loss of Bill

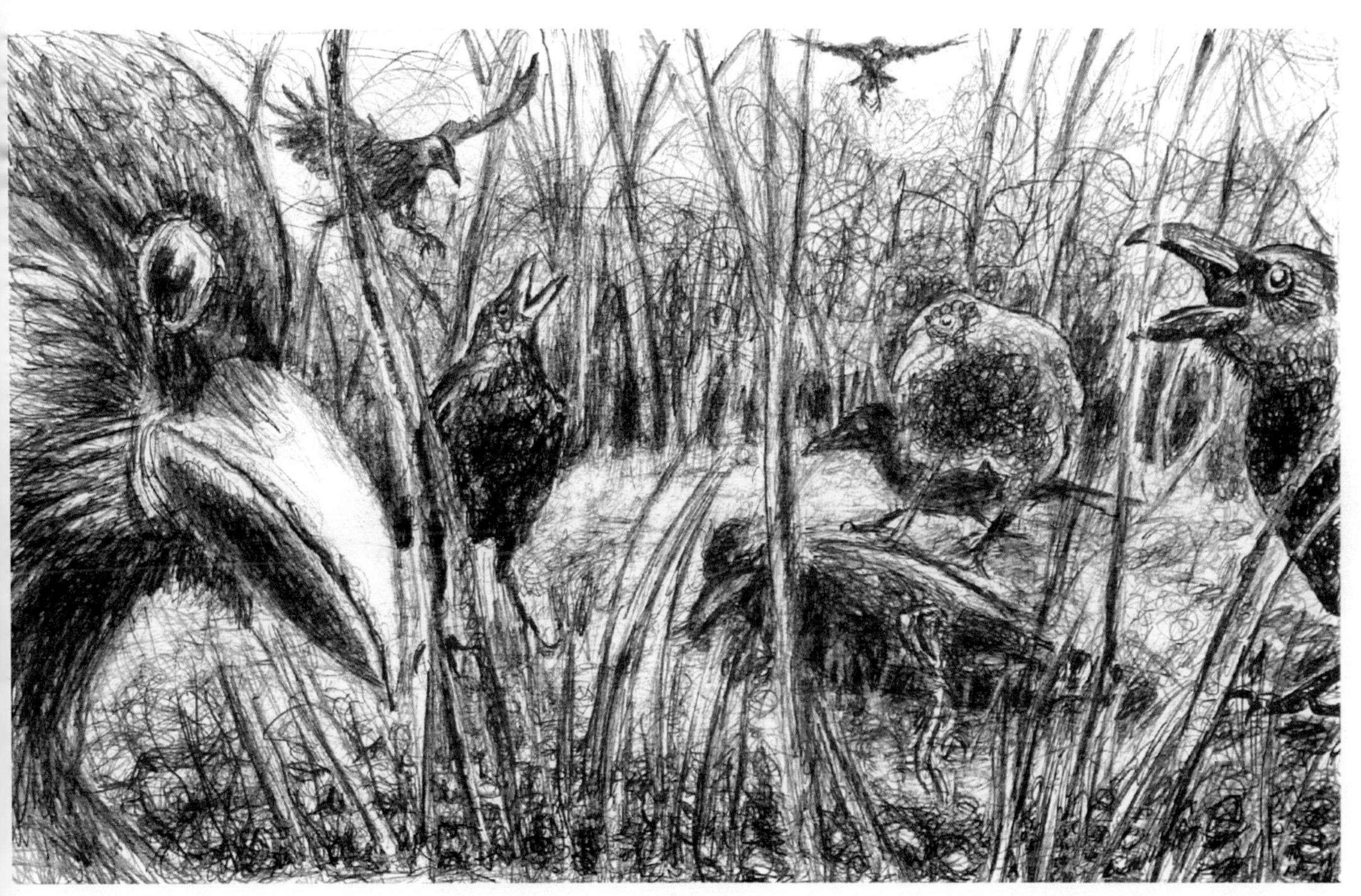

Amongst the tall grasses

Amongst the tall grasses
we gyre and wade
darlings in straw
as the hours do fade

This way and that,
curiosities abound
What is this off-taste,
what's that on the ground?

Summer's cruel heat
has left us for good,
to seek tender mercies
from the gold
'tween our feet

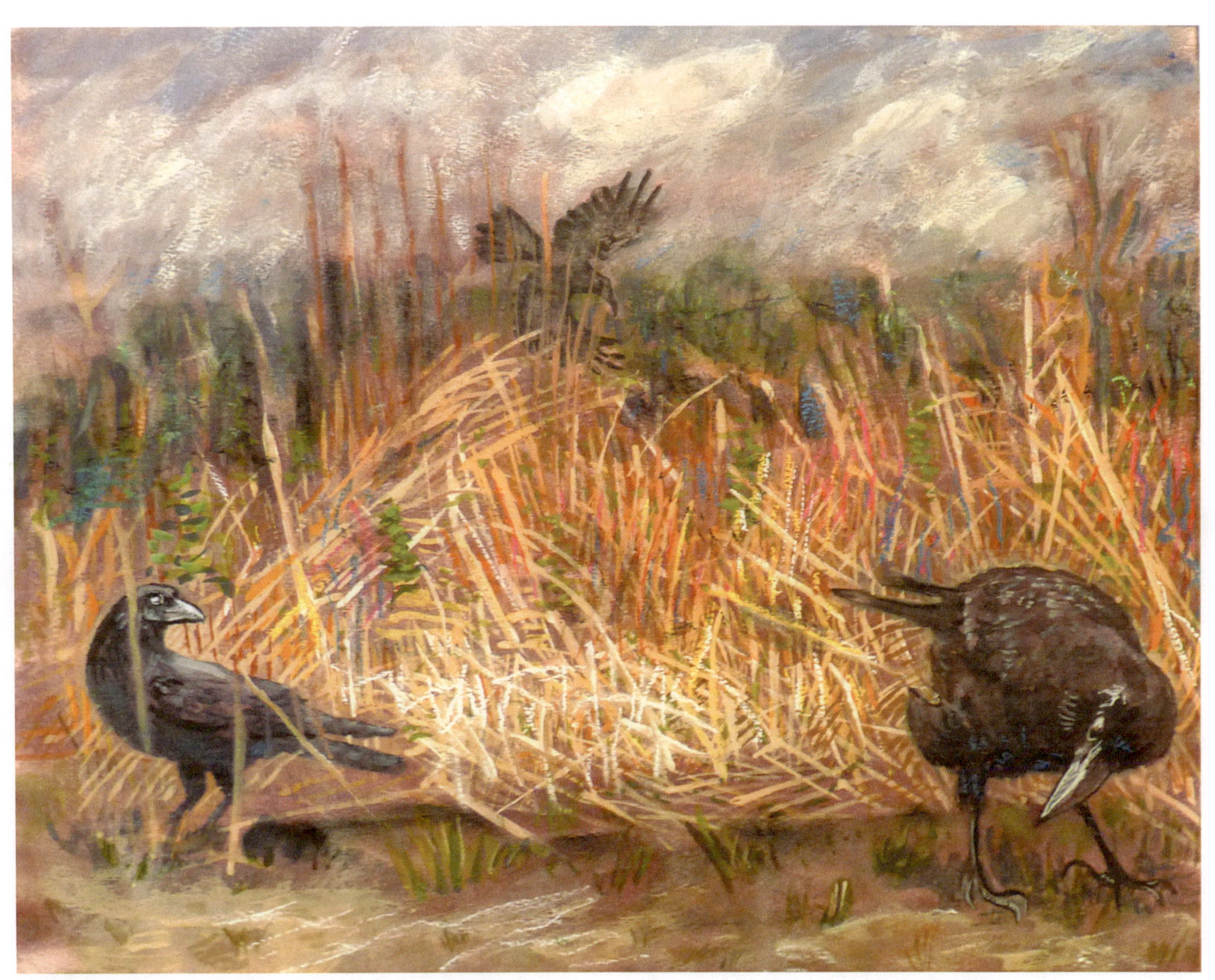

What has become of me

I've become so
strange lately
my nose has grown sharper
my eyes quite improved
my hair has descended
wild and jet-black

God knows what
my friends will think now,
And my family will
doubtless depart

My legs are too spindly
my feet long and narrow,
Oh my toes
surely dangerous,
sharpened deadly hooks

I wave my arms
and run the yard,
barely making it
off the ground.
I feel myself
getting stronger
and my voice is
becoming quite hoarse

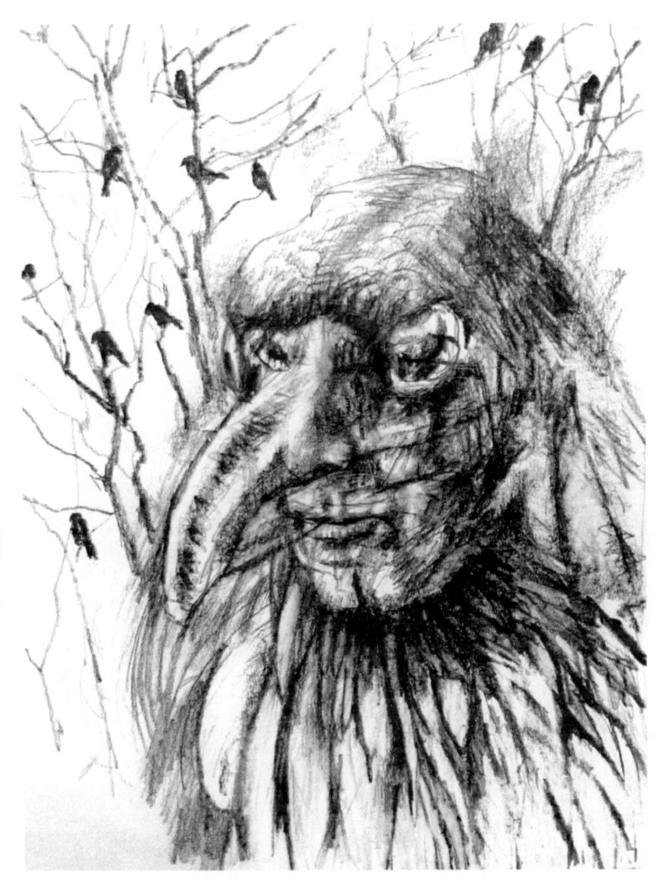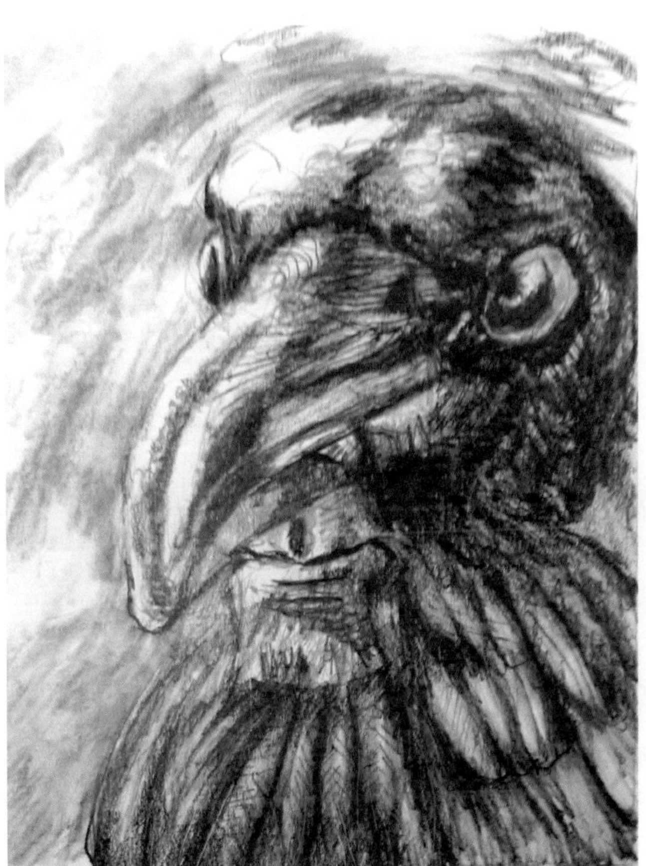

Turning the Season

This day, yes yes,
you feel it too
the last and the first,
an interlude between.
Summering is falling
not failing to Fall,
the leaves tell the tale,
come witness come be

Out here in the back
of the shadowed houses
the weather and land
conspire to change.
Once warm and bleary
from heat, pale languor,
we look to the chill
and a darkened December

But now live and sing
and hunt and gather
while the sun's in the sky
and the winds seldom roar.
We feel the signs of
the ending of summer
and straighten our wings
for cold breathing ahead

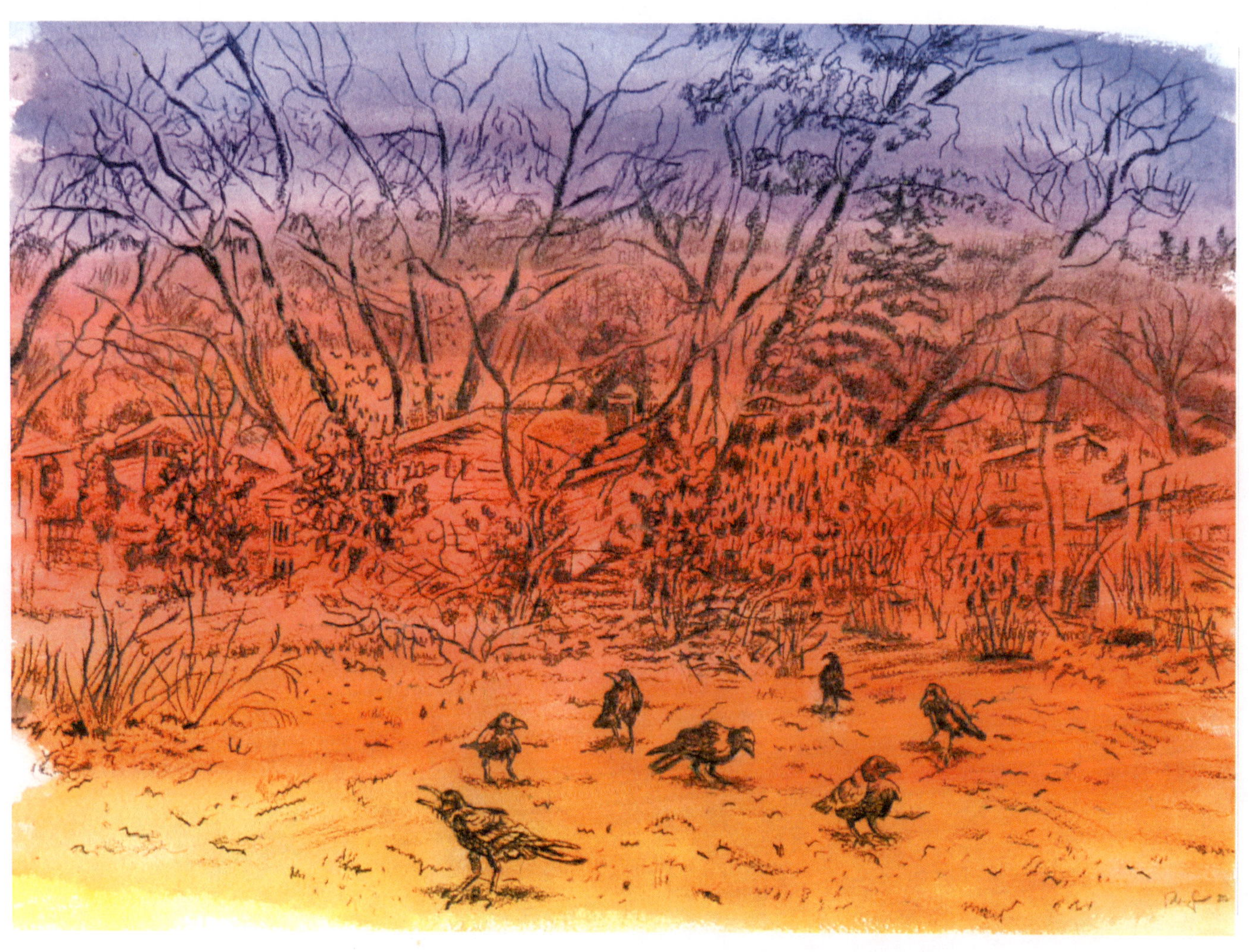

The Ritual

It's said that
in the land before Aleph,
on the highest and farthest of mountains,
those with the gift
would gather
as the sun slowly did rise

There they don their darkened feathers
and sharpen their pointed beaks,
and practice their new tongue
with delight

We weren't there
to see them aloft
and disappear from sight

But those hidden in the heathers,
and by stone and barren branch,
solemnly swear
every word is the truth.

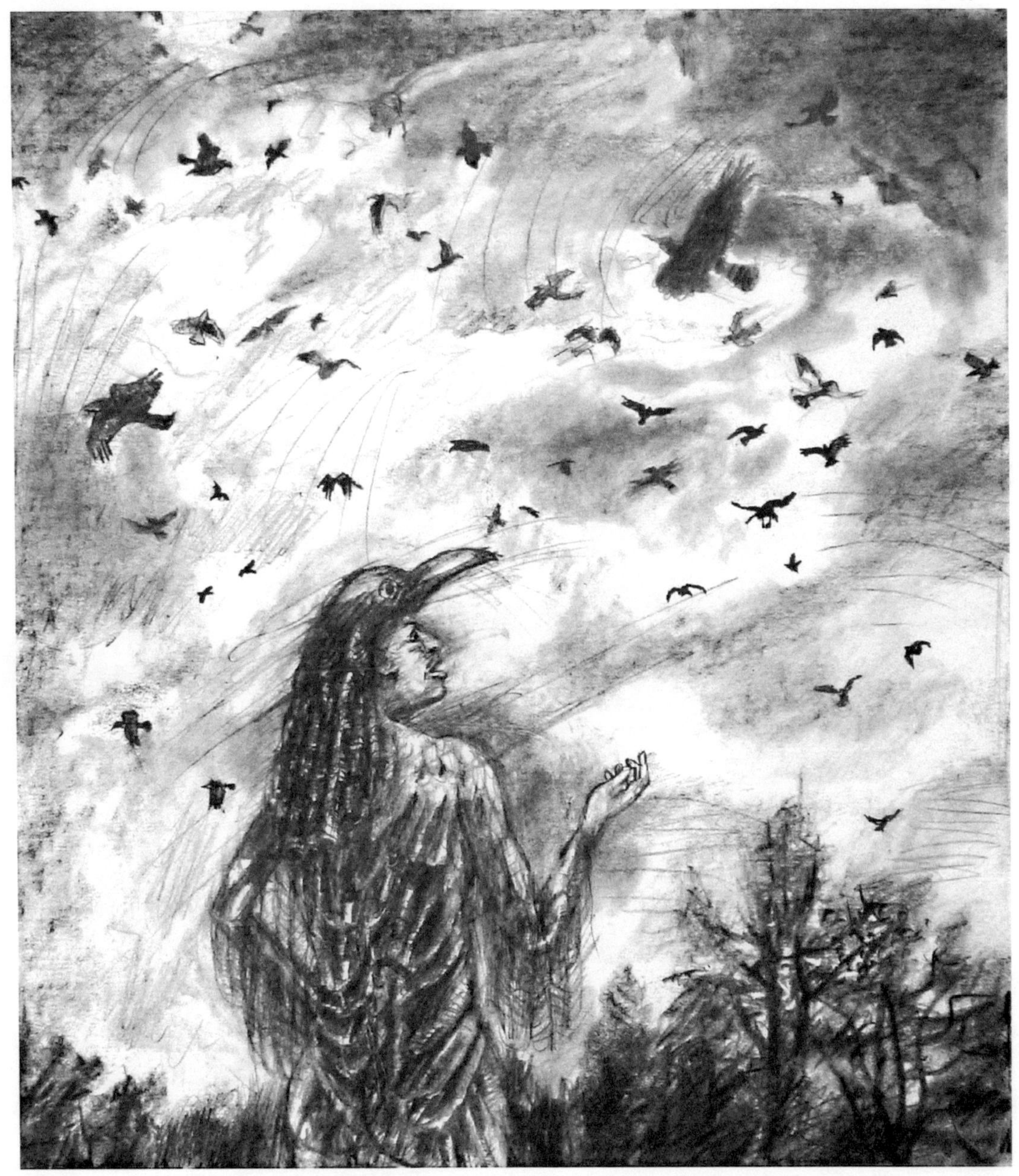

Red Vision

End of day hunger
our meal not met,
we canvas the grounds
under bloodied sky

Meadow so altered
our desire—consternation
we evolve our own fiction
to preserve our warm brain

But oh the air, oh oh so
lovely the hues,
of magenta and pink
rose cinnabar, and fertile
lush vermillion

But wonder now wait
stop pause left right pause,
Who are we now
in such a
strange bold land?

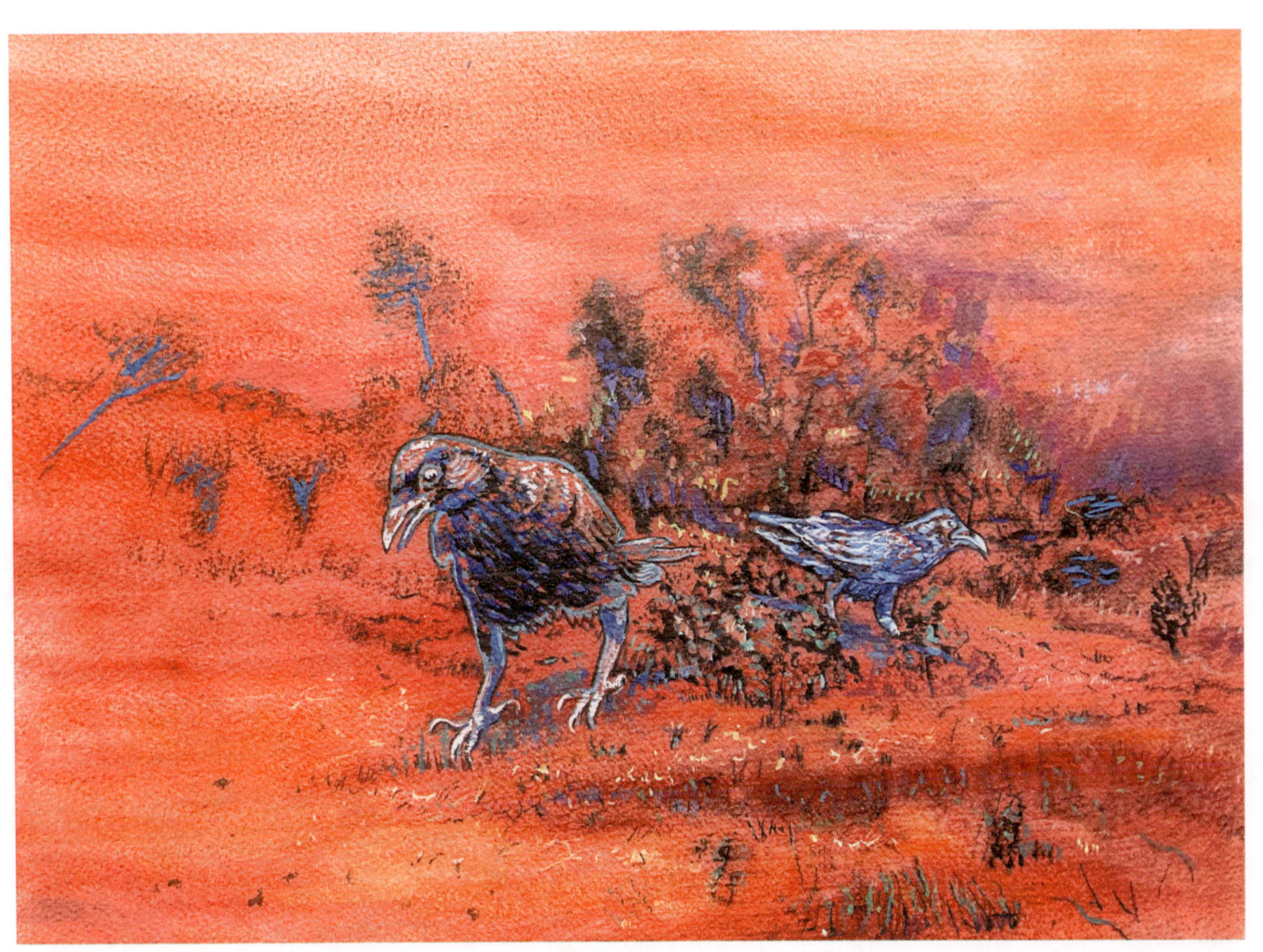

In the Wings

In the wings is where
my family abides
A grateful comfort
to know who I am

The soft wings
rush of air
the warm black
of our feathers
even the smell
is sublime

We rise and fall
roost and caw
gather to feast
and chat and coo

and turn out
the Demon hawk

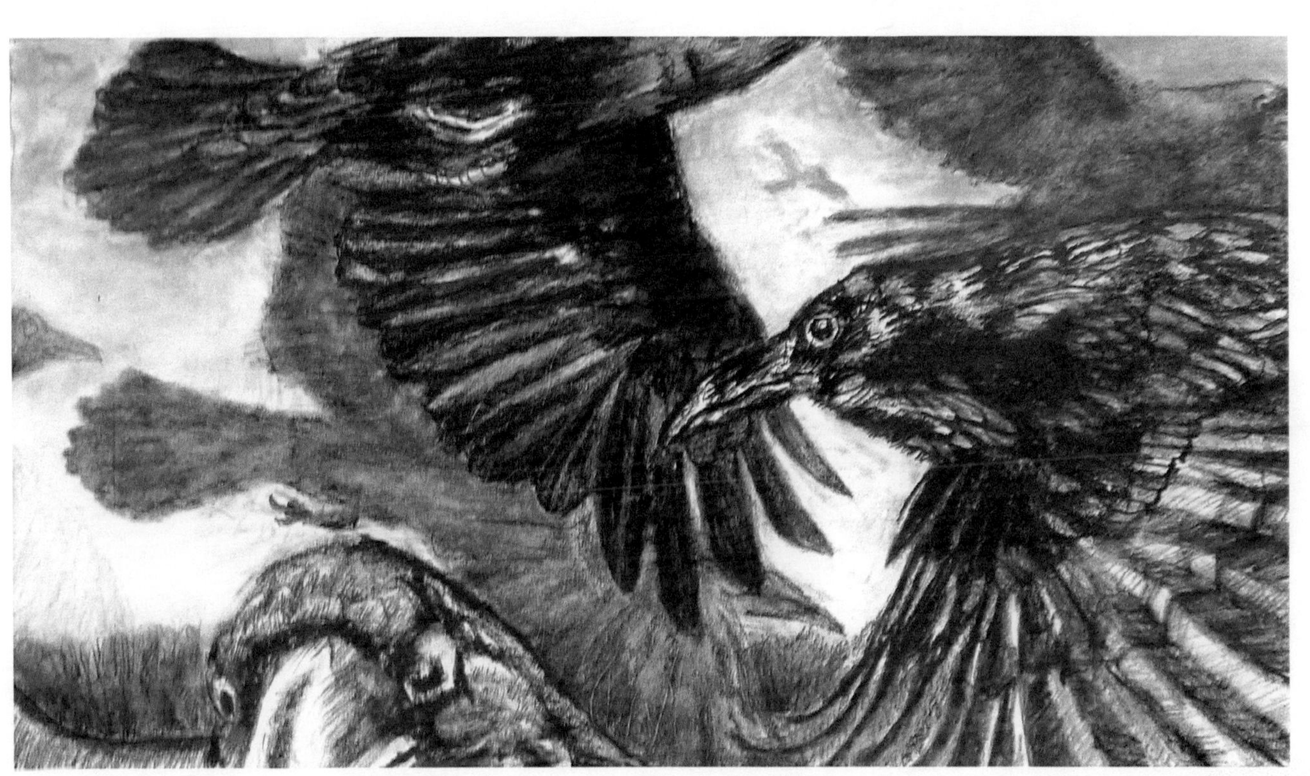

The Beast of Erdenheim

Each winter so unexpected
come the horrible avian creatures
tell us not of right or reason, but
Boschian nightmare features

Down they swoop to raucous cry
the air shudders with blue surprise
consider not the bell's alarm
for your escape from grievous harm

Take the pets but leave my person
take them away to the land of nod
this is no country for you to welcome
do your worst and then begone

Why do you appear in yearly torrents,
to snap our bones and earthly spirits?
Why does the worm consume our flesh
when winter's been too long?

Alas
raise a glass
December comes
but once a year.

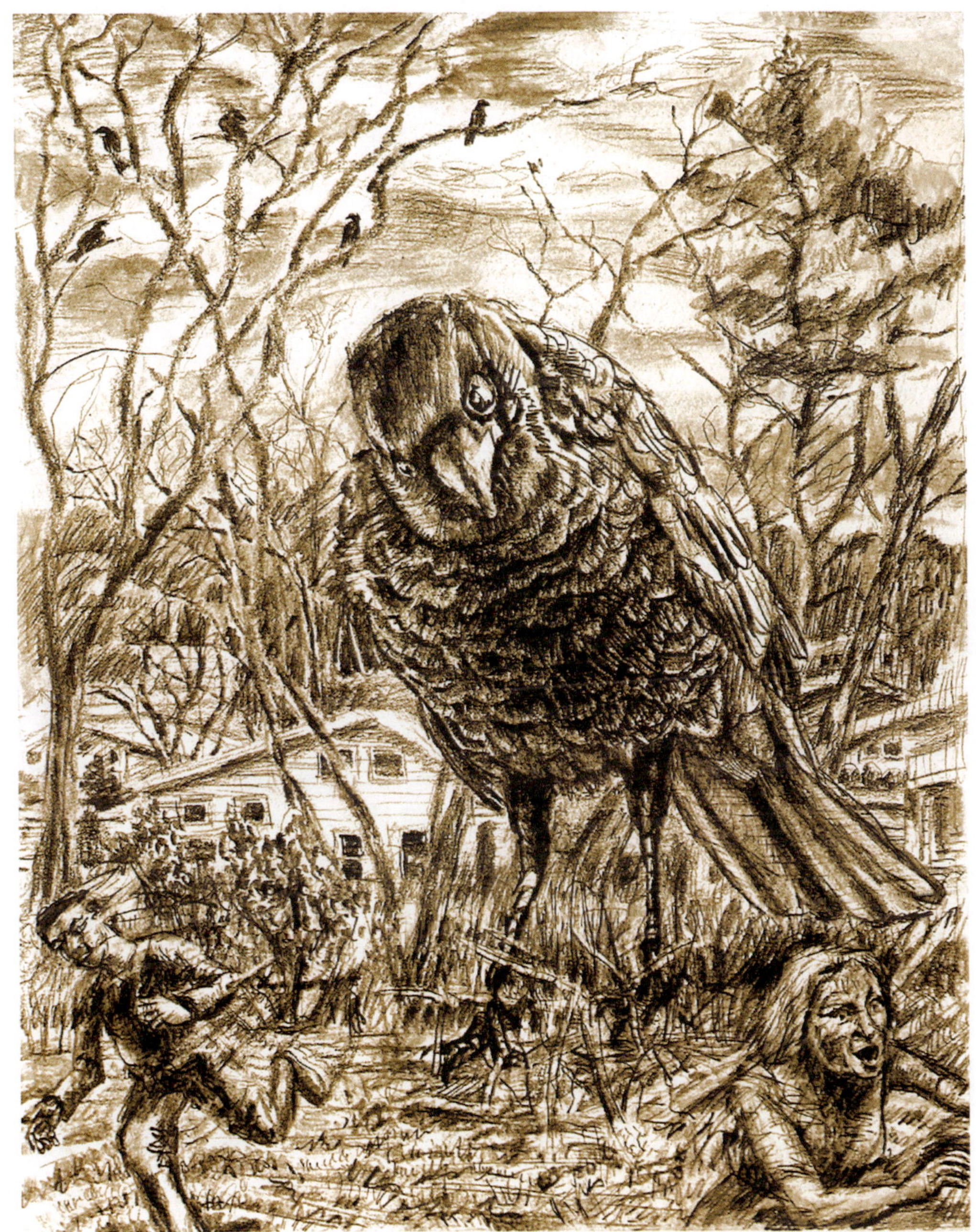

The Field

What have we here
on this fine day?
I say to my mates
with raucous smile

The scent of humans
roiling and still,
in the pungent
noontime heat

Looks like a feast
for many a day,
I say to my mates
I do

And glide we did
with hungry belly
to our appointed
undertaking.

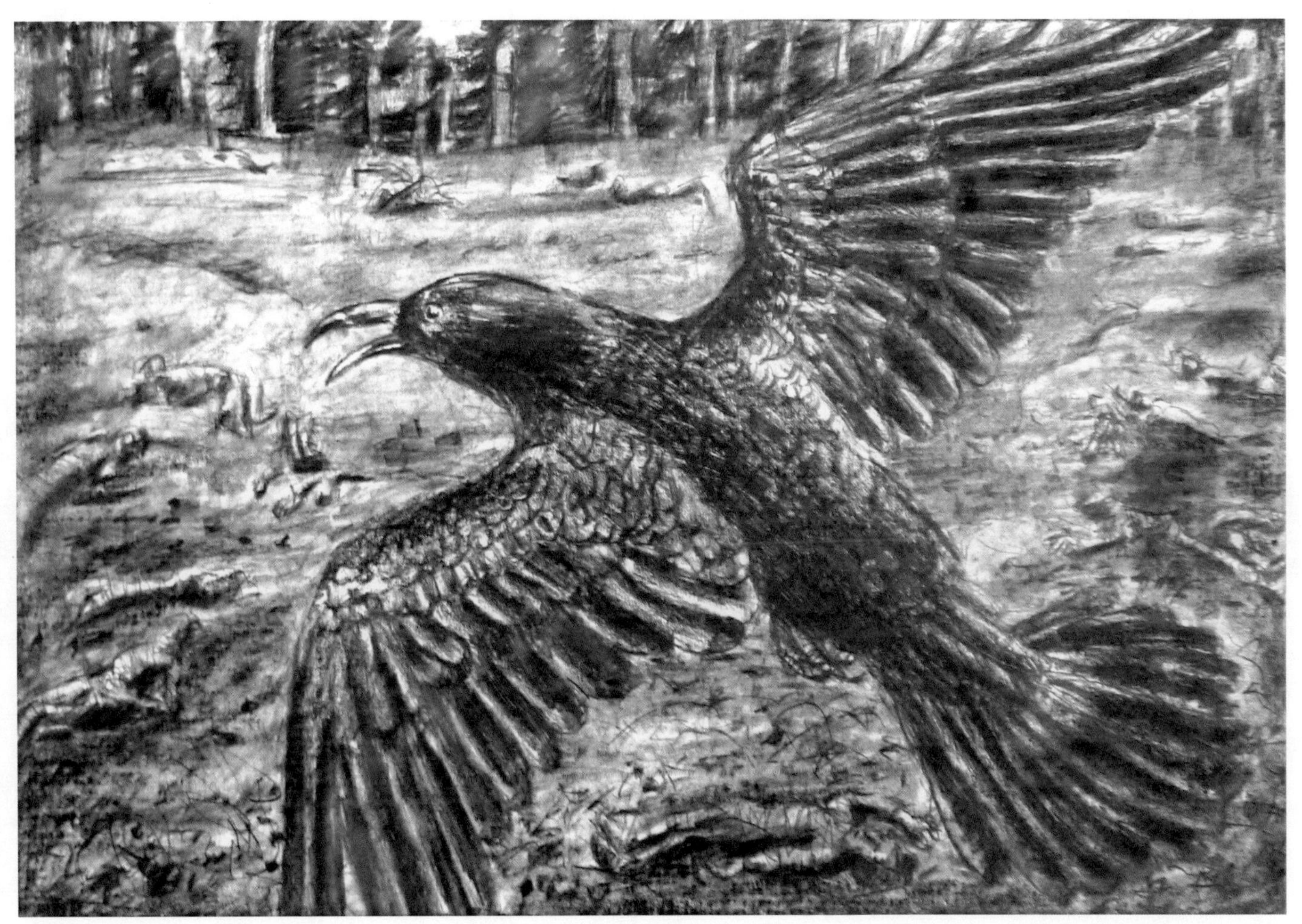

Day for Night

Who am I by day
Am I different by night
Of course and no
In the warmth of the day we fly and fill our eyes
At night we roost in the soft darkness
The day brings adventurous meals
The night, quiet murmurs with friends and family
At day, hard reality smacks us
At night one can see the spirits

Together at night
we dream strange futures
Prophesies and tragedies
shiver and collude

The place between
day and night
is my favorite of all
visions are shifting
edges blur
the mystery slowly unfolds

Some may worry as the eyes
lose touch
but in the dark roost
comfort abides

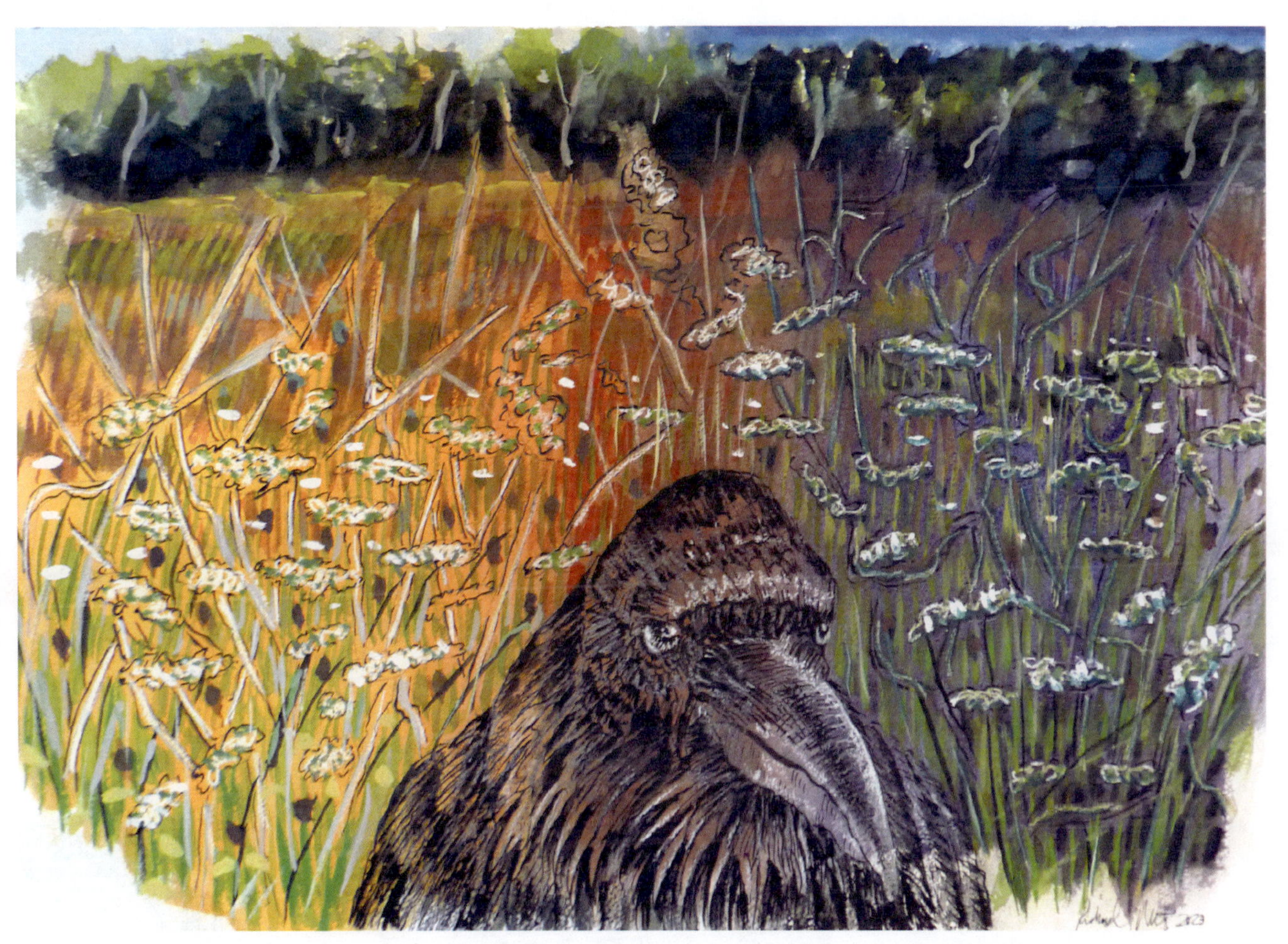

Snowstorm

A snowstorm has found us
and on we will trundle,
it's much too much
for elegant flight,
grounded now yes
for the bleaklong hours
the darkening night.
But worry not worry
my oldtrue friend
we've faced thrice more
over mountain and moon
from our first rich rasp
to wing upon wing

No colors to see
our through-way blurs snow
Sham-shickle, grouse-muddle,
discuss kin and our foe,
who's up and fearless,
who's not, like us

As the white-cold white
piles up all about,
how much longer
much longer don't say,
for best rest in our
rest-nest

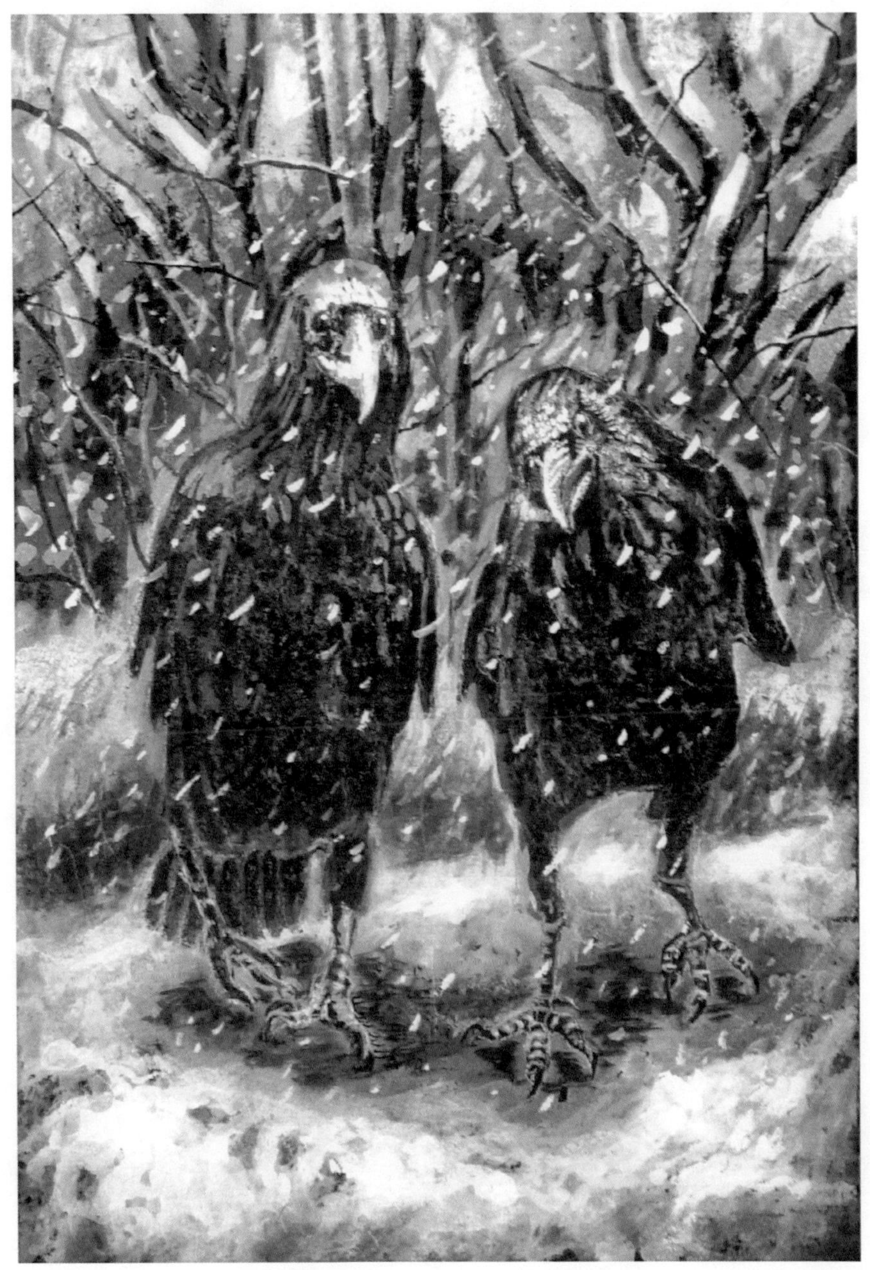

Acoustic Vibrations

How can we imagine that
even such disparate creatures:

Don't hem and haw,
and quarrel and haggle
kvetch and assent
and mumble and murmur
seduce and insult
and guide and be guided
entertain and complain
observe and inquire
propose and exclaim
tattle and proclaim,
upon this great and mysterious
planet?

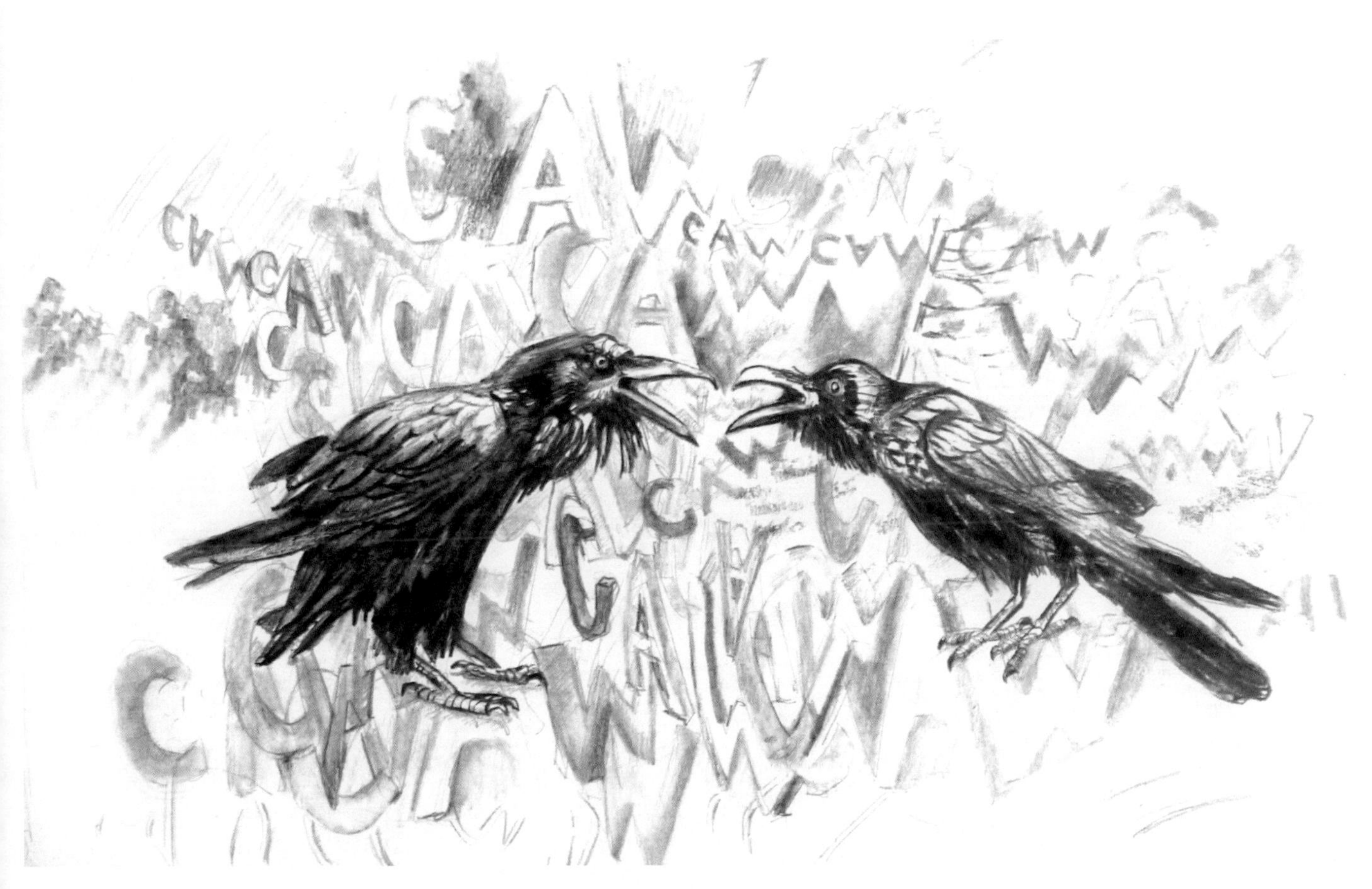

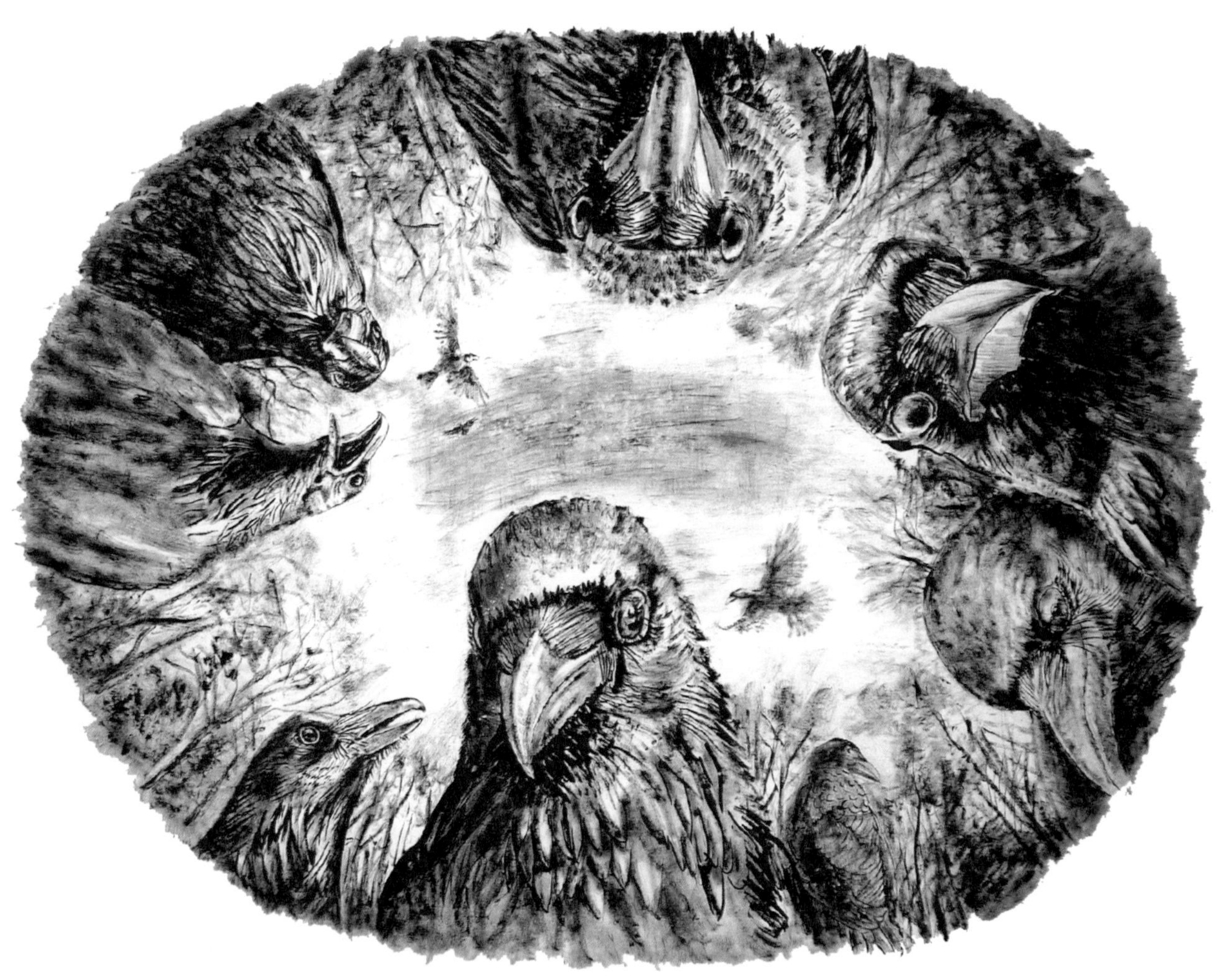

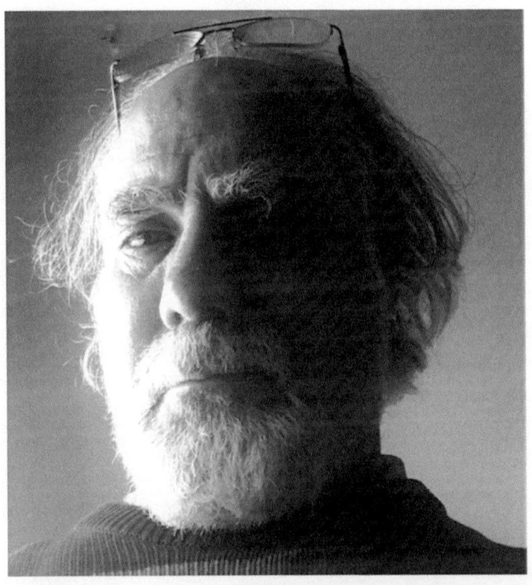

Richard Metz is a writer and artist who lives just outside Philadelphia, PA. He has been writing and making art works for forty years. He has been focusing on crows and ravens for the last five years, and has a relationship with the murder that lives in his neighborhood.

www.mistermetz.com

Thank you to Rachel Kobin and the Philly writers group, editor and publisher Alison Lewis, and my family Sam Metz, Harry Metz, and Cecilia Dougherty for being so helpful to me and my work.

9 781642 510553